SHEEP

ON THE SOMME

A World War 1
Pictures and Poetry Project

FRANK PREM

Publication Details

Title: Sheep On The Somme
ISBN: 978-1-925963-14-4 (h-bk)
ISBN: 978-1-925963-61-8 (pbk)

Published by Wild Arancini Press
2021

Sheep On The Somme - a World War 1 Pictures and Poetry Project is a collection of poems written in response to archival imagery of World War 1, and in particular, the Western Front.

All images were available under Creative Commons provisions, or otherwise free of copyright restrictions, and full attribution is provided.

Cover collage includes elements from a number of images included in this book:

AWM Accession Number E01200 https://www.awm.gov.au/collection/C43140
AWM Accession Number P10550.158 https://www.awm.gov.au/collection/C1294154
AWM Accession Number E00846 https://www.awm.gov.au/collection/C953168
AWM Accession Number E01087 https://www.awm.gov.au/collection/C54940

all we'd ever done was push cattle . . .

Contents

About
Sheep On The Somme

The genesis of *Sheep On The Somme - a World War 1 Pictures and Poetry Project* can be traced back to a single photograph, used as the cover for a WW 1 history. The book was titled *The Great War*, and written by a very fine Australian journalist, Les Carlyon (published by Macmillan in 2006. ISBN:978 1 4050 3761 7).

The image was of a devastated landscape – bombed to a slurry, with a single cross standing proud and sunlit in the middle of the ocean of grey nothing. The cross marked the grave of Captain Ivor Margetts, formerly of Tasmania, and was obliterated by further artillery strikes within a relatively short time of being erected.

That wonderful, desolate image set me on a quest to find and contemplate more, leading me through hundreds of images archived online in War Memorial Museums and State and National Libraries.

Each image had its own story to tell.

The project is very loosely divided into a number of sections, notionally presenting a beginning, middle, and an end, but there was no such organisation involved in the writing, simply responses to the image before me, and the collection of poems can be read randomly.

Enjoyment is a wrong term to use in the context of this subject, so I won't wish for that. Instead, I hope that the images might speak to you, as they did to me.

FP

welcome, welcome

for glory

hurrah!
the slouch hat
marches

hurrah!
their tramping
feet

hurrah! hurrah!
they will cover
themselves
in glory

australia sends
its best

australia
sends its best

because the king
has need
and old england
has need
and the generals
have need
of men

and men

and men

so *hurrah!*
they march to fight
for england

hurrah!
in glory
for the king

no matter where
the empire fights
australia . . .

australia

brave
brave
australia

will
be there

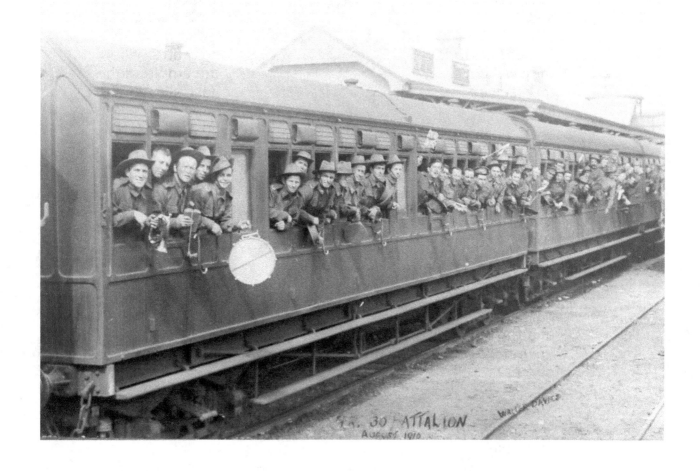

to remember (we will play)

we will play we will play	for those we leave behind to remember	those same old songs
a blast of bugle	. . .	play to remember
ta *ta ra* *ta-ra ra-ra*	and we will sing	*ta* *ta ra* *ta ra*
we will play we will play	now *sotto voce* hush your voice	
bang the drum loudly bang the drum	we will hum deep in our chests	
ta-ta *ta* *ta* *ta ta*	for the boys all the boys we leave behind	
boom	yes we will play . . .	
boom	we will play	

going somewhere

and we are
all aboard
at last

going somewhere
even if it's
just
for a fight

we all signed up
to see the world

so come on

bring it on
for us

we're from
australia
and we're
ready

12

for pride

malcolm
my boy

so well you look

in your
greatcoat
and
your slouch hat
and khaki puggaree

the rising sun
gleaming
at the side

proud of you
I am
so proud that . . .

oh
I could
almost burst
for pride

14

and serious (for mum)

come on
come on
look sensible
can't ya

I want this
to go home
to my mum

don't want her
thinking
I'm here with riff-raff
like you blokes

she'd worry

yeah
just sit there
then
will ya
and don't move

bluey
you stand the other
side

I'll go just here

come on
behave ya-selves
won't ya's

it's for mum

alright then
here we go

straight ahead
and serious

.

.

.

alright

let's go have
some fun

the strolling women (of pont d'achelles)

let us walk now
as we used
to do

before the men
and their machines

a promenade
while our trees
still stand

a gentle walk
like women
do

a stroll
to maintain
who we are

we are not
the battle
raged
beside us

we are not
the bombs

that fall behind

we are
the mothers

the wives the girls
the daughters

we are strolling
not denying

being
what we will need
to be
should we
somehow
survive

unease (until they go)

what is this
thing
happening
everywhere

who are these
men
in uniform

so drab

they come
and go
then
come again

frighten the horses
the pigs
and the farrowing sow

covet
my cockerel
that cheeky small bird
each time
he crows

how long
such foolishness

I wonder

but
I hear the roar
and feel the thunder
in my bones

these are
poor signs
that bode
nothing good

and I do not
know

I do not know

but
what I feel
is *uneasy*

yes

uneasy

each time
I see more of them
go past

hurry (they come)

you must leave

you must
go

they are coming
yes
they come

take your cart
your horse

take
grand-mère
and all your food

then hurry
you must go

for
they are coming

yes

they come

sister (photograph)

we are just
boys
we are *just* men

we've popped over
to help settle
a fuss

come
little girl
I've a sister
at home

not very different
to you

come
be one of us
for an instant

a lifetime

one hundred years

a photograph

and I will
recall
to my dying day

that there are sisters
to me
around the world

that all
round this
conflicted world
there are girls
who could be
my
little sister

for a romp

somewhere
on the journey

   my horse . . .

   my hat . . .

somewhere
along the way
we must have turned
an egyptian direction

so I'll
salute the sphinx
climb the pyramid
carve my name
in capital letters

into them both

take a gallop
across the loose sand

but
hold the hump

keep hold
(for gawd's sake)
of the hump

end the day
back in cairo

back
in cairo -
don't tell my mother -
for a romp

(so very) old and (so very) young

grand-père
grand-mère

may we play
before
we work

the fields
will surely
wait
a little while

~

grand-père
grand-mère

will we plant
today

did we plough
enough
yesterday
to take the seed
from us

to grow

~

grand-père
grand-mère

should we cut
this bread
less wide

if we slice it
thin enough
perhaps . . .

for supper

~

grand-père
grand-mère

let me help
you
with the linen

with the bowls
and with
the plates

perhaps we
might
need them
where we go

~

grand-mère
grand-mère

let me dig
this
deepest hole

I am young
but
you know
how strong I am

I
will cover him

28

making a home

a shovel

some burlap sacks

I will dig
my home

I will sack it

reinforce it

I will make a hole
in the ground
that a man
like me
might live in

and a spade

here we are
in our new
home

we hope
to be here
for awhile

do you like
our small household
improvements

there is
nothing
that can't be achieved
with broken wood
some hessian sacks
and
a spade

pay you (a winkle)

how much
lady

how much
for all the winkles
in your basket

scoop
them up
scoop them up

your mule
is a witness

and the old man
doesn't care

scoop them into
my bowl

I
will pay you

soon (would you like a cup of tea?)

cup of tea?

my wife and I
always
had a cup of tea
at eleven

not such a stew
as this one
but
I'll take
what I can

it's nice to have
a break
even a short one
with the boys

back again
soon enough

.

.

.

too soon

too soon

the best day

that bike
my bike
is a
lean
machine

it's slender
and it's fast

but I can't
ride
above a slippery mile
for the mud
that's trying
to bring me
down

so
I clean my machine
every minute
of the day
every minute
that I'm
not riding

a bit of cloth
a bit of stick

a bit
of elbow
grease

to clean that mud
away

one day
the sun is going
to shine

that day
will be
the best

because
the mud
will dry
and
on the road
I'm going to be flying

one sweet day

the best

25 — ALBERT (Somme) - Le petit Dermancourt. Vue prise avant le bombardement
General view.

G. Lelong, 21, Rue St-Martin, Amiens

pretty place

a pretty place
albert

such
a pretty place

to see it . . .

green fields
town buildings
and a church
up on the hill

to see it
you could imagine . . .

ararat
or horsham

you could
imagine
some sort of life

you could believe
it might come through
unscathed

a pretty place

yes

I wish it well

358 — FRICOURT (Somme) - La Gare — The Railway station

G. Lelong, 21, rue St-Martin, Amiens

40

who could imagine (in 1913)

it seemed like   no one
nothing   of us
could touch us   could
in 1913   imagine

we were nothing

uninvolved

only a place
of small farms

a little
wheat

and chickens

a railway line

yes
perhaps a problem
with the railway
line

but
in 1913
who could imagine

easier (should be)

here we are
in from gallipoli

here we are
we survived

this time
maybe
we get to *achieve*
something

not like
where we were

huddled
on the low ground
so the turks could
pick us
off

I hear that
where we're going
is all flat ground

should be
an easier place
to fight

ok (we were)

hell jimmy

it would have been
better
if we'd stayed
in cairo

you and me
and the fleshpots

we did okay

the pyramids
were real

the sphinx was full
of questions

and you and me
under the clear skies
and the stars

we were doing
no harm
to anyone

ah jimmy

we were doing
okay

one cuppa (a week)

thank god
for a cuppa

I'm parched

it's a slog
in the mud
out there

bullets are flying
and the bombs shriek
all the time

and
it's boring as hell
just waiting

a fag
in the trenches
and a game
of catching lice
is as much
entertainment
as we can manage

thank god
for your cuppa
and now I'm off
back
to the frontline

I'll see you
in a week
if I make it

marching (closer)

marching

if we're not
sitting
in a trench
with our bums
in the wet

we're marching

or waiting
in the pitch black
of night
for the shrill
and the whistle
and the bright
flash
of the burst
that tells us
they missed

so we can go
right on
with our marching
to some different
sector

and some different
trench
but the same
bloody water

and the same rats
and lice

and the same shriek
of death
that

this time

might fall
much closer

captured (in a photograph)

let us rest with you
a while

we will do no harm

we are just
shadows

a noise
passing in front
of your light

silhouettes
against the sun

while you
are the peace we crave
set
in a calm
reflection

photograph . . .

I will take
a photograph
of you

one day

someone may see it
and recall

there were signs
of spring
showing –
just enough -
to test
if the weather
is warm

but
don't trust
in seasons
anymore

and do not
trust
in men
who are shadows
passing

I have this moment
for all time

captured
in a photograph

safe (until)

line us up
like sardines
in a tin

we'll be safe enough
tonight

until the spotters
see our tents

until the front
advances

until we're told
to pack all
of our kit

and move out
toward
the lines

every breath a hope

when I left
for this

I was a fool
to hope

but the picture
I carried demanded
hope
of me

and
though I fight
with will
and I believe
the cause

still
I carry
my hope

with every breath
I take

we'll send him clean

I suppose he died
like any of us
die
here

in the mud

doing his job

they don't issue
exemptions
you know
just because
you're not carrying
a rifle

and a bomb
doesn't know
that you're looking
for survivors

no bomb knows
that you're there

it just whistles
and it shrills
and it frightens you

so you're dead
almost
before it explodes

I suppose
that he died
just like any of us
could die

in a dirty damn way

but
we'll bury him
as friends should bury
when they must

we'll send him
sad
and deep
and clean

lost (as I am)

johnny johnny
I wonder
did you
really
have to go

what seemed so *real*

and so *urgent*
in nineteen sixteen
has become
a vacant space

a hole
in our lives
forever

and I wonder
johnny

in the long evenings
I wonder . . .

the baby
doesn't cry
in the night
anymore

and young colin
is growing
into a fine young man

you'd be proud
I know

but this street
of ours
is in mourning

you are not
the only one
to have fallen
in the fields
over there

I hope
that they gave you
a burial

it would be hard
to think of you
abandoned

or lost

(as I am lost
my johnny)

sheep on the somme

lambs
to slaughter
freezing

diggers
in coats of wool

have you ever
seen it cold
like this

the western district
cockies
can be hard on a man
don't you know

but
they wouldn't leave
a sheep
outside
near this winter

nowhere near
this winter
somme

pausing (while I rest)

sandbags
to the ceiling

having a rest
propping up the wall

it's a crazy war
when there's nothing
to do
on a rest break

ypres
has turned out
rather dull

no fleshpots here
like cairo

god
don't I wish
that I
was still
in cairo

instead of holding up
a rotten wall

just like the gods
are holding up
the rotten war

waiting until I feel
rested enough
to re-join them
in battle

this war (by bike)

this war
is child's play

somewhere
I left my boots
behind

never mind
my dirty hut
little more
than
an open lean-to

and never mind
my pants
being too short

there might be water
near
but I won't need
bathing gear

I will ride my bike
right
into the waves

winner

come in spinner

there's pennies
on the kip

throw them
high

make them
spin

heads come down
I'm
a winner

head
still on

winner

pudding on christmas

merry christmas
sir

now
how can we help you
today?

a little family get together
this evening?

well, I have
a very special
rate
for these plum puddings
just in
from *home*

some marmalade
perhaps?

very well
sir

thank you
sir

enjoy
your pudding
sir

damper and

let the dixie
boil

clear the water
of whatever
is *in* the water
here
in the kitchen
of dickebusch

if we get a pinch of flour
we can
at least
scratch out a bit
of damper

and a cup
of tea

jalopied heart

yesterday
passes
to the right

harnessed
to its buggy

while the motorcade
of today
passes
on the left

keeping closely
to the kerb

every body
to the curb

lest the jalopies
running down
tomorrow
wish to claim
the cobbled heart

74

lost robbie

ah robbie

paschendale claimed you
at the last

was it
at the menin road ridge

was it playing
leap-frog
in the advance

ah robbie
we didn't even know
we'd lost you

but
when we did . . .

we couldn't even find
ourselves

when we met (on herberg street)

take
a bus
down herberg street

do some window
shopping
in the rain

there's no rush
and you can take
as much time
as you need

but
mind now
how you go
out there

keep the cobbles
beneath
your wheels

it's a glue pot
on the other side

and if you stray
you might be *gone*
so
keep it narrow

keep it
on the road

and I'll see you
again
in just a day
or two

over the top
or
in the mire

either way
I'll watch out
for you

and remember

we once met
on herberg street

78

one to take care (of his grieving mother)

jimmy
did you hear the news

your young johnny
died

I didn't hear
the how
but
it was just a month
ago

tom took a shot
to his face
and lambert
got a wound
in the hand

but your other lad
job
will be sent home
to take care
of his grieving mother

it will be
the lot
of job
to take care
of his grieving
mother

welcome (welcome)

welcome
to hell

this is
the place

all things
are broken
here

crippled
splintered
betrayed

we welcome
you
to hell

is it a
visit

will you stay

so many
think
the one
but
their minds get
changed

do you remember
when . . .

can you look back
so far

I think
those days are past

you
will carry this *now*
until your days
are done

a swamp
of all the world

commanders? I do not think so

are you walking
to the front
marshal joffre?

general haig?

come along
we'll show you
where
the heat is

down by suicide-corner
. . .

accidents occur

and you can bet
the bloody bosche
know
how to shoot

no

not there for a
commander

I don't think
so

or
would you listen

maybe
from beside the guns
general haig?

only
they will have
your ears
over-full of blood
before you know it

and you
will have to read me
because you won't
hear
a word

no

not there
either
for a commander

I do not think
so

marshal joffre
inside the ambulance?

although
the screaming
and the moans
could complicate
detailed planning

so . . .

no

not there for a
commander

I really
do not think
so

I suppose
that leaves the choice
of muddy trenches

would you stand . . .

would you

clamber . . .

would you crawl
all that way
just
to see us?

no no
not there
for our commanders

I really
really
do not think so

we need to keep you
safe
and we need you
thinking clear

the bosche
are up to tricks
again
and we need you
to stay
well away
in the rear

a corpse: a crop (mouquet farm 1)

what is the sound
of
the naked earth

can you hear
the horizon line

sticks

sticks
that were a forest once

sticks

these sticks
that were a home

ghosts
and brown water
fill
the shell holes

ghosts and bones
and rising smoke

plough this field

a crop
of corpse

plough it smooth
when war has . . .

.
.
.

stop
a moment

let your head bow
low

think of what was once
the mouquet farm

then
plough the field
remove the splinters
smooth the mounds

forget you ever stood
on mouquet farm

a corpse
a crop

the seasons pass

a crop

a corpse

that season
past

come the morning (mouquet farm 2)

a cup
of soup?

I've boiled the bones

dip your pannikin
deeply

arms
and legs
and sundry joints

a broth
incendiary
waits you

~

what is it
ails?

your appetite
gone?

never mind
sleep tight
sleep deep
until tomorrow

we'll serve some more
fresh flesh

new stock

I am sure
you will feel
better
come the morning

mountains until (mouquet farm 3)

these sticks
will be the last
matchstick forest

these mounds
will be my mountains
until . . .

I have fallen
and I
have fallen

a crater of bed
a midden
of blanket

these mounds will be
my mountains

until

trenchant plans

a cut
above

no mud
lies here

our trenches
might well
win the war
for us

it was our plan
our well-thought-out
plan

to be above
the bog
while our enemy
flounders

a good plan -
such
a good plan -
we will see
in a while
how it holds up

when the shells
begin
to dance

poor ivor (1)

let us sing
a song

for ivor margetts

a captain
of tasmania
he was

fair for france
fair
for dying

ivor sailed
and
ivor led

did someone
weep

poor ivor
is dead

Over the top, amid bursting gas and tear shells, in a determined assault on the fortified Somme villages.

run (fortified)

up
through the poison fog

up
into the bullet
rain

over the top
and run
right at them

don't take
your mask off

don't stop

to cough
your breath

mustard gas
will claim
your lungs

tear gas will blind
your eyes

and right now
you're going to need
to see
what's coming

no time (*giddap*)

giddap

let's move along

there are bodies
alive
to take away
from the lines

giddap
giddap

there is no time
to lose

death
is at our shoulders
but we might
be fast enough
if we . . .

come on
all of you
idling

mount up
onto your wagons

there is no time
to lose

giddap

clip clop (stay alive)

I am
the ambulance

I drive (*clip clop*)
on pitted paths

the dugouts
beside the road
show that
the war has been

but
I do not fight
I
gather up
the pieces

all
the little
broken
pieces

put them together
beneath a bandage

and hope they'll heal

while I run
to get another

and I run
to stay alive

then I pack us
all
in the wagon

(*clip clop*)

(*clip clop*)

move along

catch my breath

I stay alive

500 yards (north of montauban) (mon-tar-ben)

they call the place
la boisselle (**la bos-ell**)

and they call it
quarry siding

somewhere near pozieres (**pozi-air**)
was where I saw it . . .

where I saw him

it happened
around albert

over by bapaume (**ba-po-m**)
or
favreuil (**fav-roy**)

it was there

somewhere over there

I last saw him
by his tent
standing

106

two pennies up (for the ambulance)

the ambulance
is
one man short

there's nothing
to be done
about that

harry
won't be serving
anymore

he's at his peace

at least
I suppose that's so

more peace for him
than for us
that's for sure

there's no point
though
in being maudlin

someone
must take up
his side
of the stretcher

it's either
you
or me

so let's toss two
pennies
high

and call it

heads

or *tails*

or *ewan*

108

not west australia

staff sergeant
is it cold
outside

do you have your
winter
leggings

have you covered
your ears
over
against the cold

so cold

staff sergeant
is snow
not
better
than the wetter months

when the water
seeps
inside your shoes

do you rub
your hands
together
inside the tent

friction
to keep them
warm

while you squirm
under a blanket
thin

with only numbness
to beat
the cold

staff sergeant
be at ease
for now

the guns
are frozen
over

marvel
at the snow
you never saw
back in west australia

back home

poor ivor (2)

has anybody
seen
poor ivor

I think . . .

I fear
the very worst

has anybody . . .

no one . . .

poor ivor

didn't he run
leading
into the charnel

did I not see him
among his troop-mates
there

in and out
amongst
the potholes
that belong to no man

I see him

yes
I think
I see him

there

the un-pock game (let's bomb ypres)

shall we play
a game

just
a small game
between
you and I

shall we see
if -
around the line -

we can fill
the picture up
entire
with a pattern
of pinholes

fill
the photograph
with the marks
of our exploded bombs

to see
if . . .

when we
are done

will anything
be left untouched

anything
un-pocked

and un-diseased

staccato

baby baby
go to sleep

I will sing
staccato

an intermittent song
I weep

through all the night
bravado

broadside on
and broadside
gone

I'll sing you
near

.
.
.

then I will sing
you

.
.
.

there

so
baby baby
go to sleep

I will sing
for you

staccato

hush

hush

be quiet now

don't . . .

do not speak
a word

if we
lay still
enough

they may not
see us

hear us

they may not
find us

oh
let them leave us
I have had
enough

too many fears

too much
explosion

cover me
cover me

I
will cover *you*

lie quiet my dear
and close

and hush

if you only hush now

they may
not
see us

rabbit hole

what are the odds
on a shell landing
where a shell
has already hit

out here . . .

well
you'd have to say
there's a chance

because
they send them over
every half minute
or so
and one day . . .

yes
one day
but
in the meantime
it's mud out
to the left

in the meantime
it's sandbags
to the right

and we dry
our burrow
until -
like rabbits
back home
on the station -

we are cosy
as can be
in a little hole

another night (like this)

and I
who wish
only
to sleep

I who would
the darkness
pray
take him

take him to
some other place

take him away

am doomed
to watch
the night at play

doomed to hear
the whistling
song

to sing it
like a mantra playing
oh god

oh god

I wonder
how long
until the sun might rise

I wonder
will it seem
much better

I wonder
if I can survive
the coming day
just to live another
night
like this

oh god

like this

wondering (and bullets)

in the darkness
we wait

hear the noise
of the distant
shells

hear the barrage
creep close

sometimes
close enough
that this concrete
shakes

and inside myself
I vibrate
in sympathy

my post
is beside my gun

my job
is to shoot

to fire

and fire and fire
and fire
again

until no men
remain

but sometimes
I walk
away

sometimes I
feel

that I need
to breathe

sometimes I gaze
at the light
on the stairs

and I wonder

all I can do
is wonder

once (like lightning)

once
I saw
lightning
strike and smite
a tree
out near the simpson
desert

the only tree
anywhere around

it exploded
in the night
and I never thought
I'd hear a noise like it
ever again

every night
is the same here

pitch black
night
and
pitch black noise

and the flash
of that tree
exploding
away on the horizon

over and over
again

sometimes . . .

sometimes
it's closer

more like
a tree
that I happen
to be standing
right underneath

would the guns might kiss

would that every
gun
would smite down
every gun

so rarely
do they kiss
each other

but chaos
yes
comes easy

and in a moment
the life
of once

is
gone

duck (the winter mud)

the accoutrements
of war
in damp
and soggy
places

who would have
thought
winning
and losing

come down
to a length
or two
of duckboard

officers
in charge
of *materiel*
assemble
the means
of battle

not guns
no

not bullets
not shells

not grenades or mines
nor needled
bayonets

we need a footpath

some way
for the boys
to walk

we cannot have
a battle

nothing like
a splendid battle
if the boys

those bonny boys
drown
in the ypres
winter mud

marching gear

we will carry
out footings
for mile
on mile

they say
an army
marches
on its stomach

this one
carries
its marching gear
on its back

while its dry

for the wet

hidden (by smoke)

I carry
the road
on my shoulder

and wonder
what path yet
I might tread

home
lies somewhere
behind me

hidden in the smoke
buried in the mud

tomorrow
lies
somewhere ahead

hidden by the smoke
(perhaps *I'm*)
buried
in the mud

but I know
the road
is a burden
upon my shoulder

somewhere ahead
hidden in the smoke
I'll lay it down

resting
riding
on the mud
until I
lay me down

12,943.   THE GREAT WAR.   Reconstructing a bridge over The Somme,
Near PERONNE.   (Copyright)

with a duckboard

from this mire
of trench-foot
sludge
and consuming swamp

drag me up
drag me out

lie me down
on the duckboard

run it across
my dear mate's head

put it
flat
upon the enemy

make it cover over
everything
this place has been
so far

a swamp (of all the world)

do not
say
a word

our comrades
are sleeping

the enemy
is near

and the forest
is breathing
a foggy spell

do not say
anything

the atmosphere
is brooding

and one false ripple
might
break the charm
of calmness
in this place

three times blessed
by the whistling
of bombs

by the tickle of a rill

a stream

of a river

into this feverish
swamp

of all the blood
ever shed
in
the world

hit the plume

even ambo's
need to take
a blow
sometimes

parked in wherever
is the lee side
to
wherever is
the fighting

they can't hit
what they can't see

unless
they're lucky

and *we*
are unlucky

meanwhile . . .

meanwhile
a smoke

let them spot
the plume of blue
and grey

hit that
if they can

a bullseye of boredom

their artillery
is bored
today

I think they decided
just to
fill
the time

to knock down
every wall
still standing

shot
by shot
to find the range

mark
after mark
by
the spotter

calling it in
to tell them

up a little bit

or
left a little bit

or bullseye

bullseye

bullseye

until
there's no wall
left
to strike

of what was

there are ruins
yet
to bomb

and *we*
are ruins
of what once was

we came
unconquerable

but somehow
we laid down
and died

maybe
we were reckless
I know some might say
that's so

yet we were not
the ones that ordered
we should go

ah well
there are ruins
left
to shell

and we
are ruins
of what was

rolling (bread and wine)

come to me
little children

I will give you
bread
and wine

come to me
little children
I will give you my bread
and a small sip
of wine

I roll your way
to bring you
this day's bread
and a spill
of your
blood red wine

an orchard (full of apples)

they reckon this place
used to be
an orchard

huh

well . . .

maybe . . .

once

anyway
let's get this thing
fixed

then
we can lob over
a few apples

a dolour a day

ah
dolorous day

we meet again

two by two
marching
into trouble

perhaps -
stretcher-laden -
three
coming back home

perhaps
one

perhaps
none

ah
dolorous day

I meet you
again

(ghost of) a chance

is there the ghost
nearby
of a medic
please

I have the ghost
of a wound
that I hold
as though for
dear life

an apparition
of a stretcher
borne by
two ambulance corpsmen

might be
my ghost
of a chance

it might be
my ghost
haunting this war

POST CARD
Daily Mail BATTLE PICTURES

These are the men who shortly after
midnight of Sunday, July 23, 1916,
took Pozières by a splendidly dashing
advance through shrapnel, shell, and
machine-gun fire.

For Address only

should I fall . . .

Printed in England

home abandoned (spirit gone)

there is no
one
home

they are gone

they are
in the backyard

a cross -
two planks of wood
placed
in the ground -
tells us
they are not here
now

their spirit
blasted high
and far away

nobody
is at home

not now

no
not evermore

sweet mary (come straight down)

sweet mary
what has happened
to you

struck by a bomb
so carelessly hurled
into the sky

do they not
know
what goes straight up
must
come straight down

do they not know
your spirit
lives on
though you cannot
see the world
as you did before

do they not understand
that a spiritual man
will still pray

still pray
to you

cathedral (my heart)

perhaps god
is always
the first to go

the target
of those who
believe only
in themselves

perhaps faith
can no more
be
the crutch
it once was

though god knows
I pray
in the cathedral
my heart

bow my head

it is here
they come . . .

they *came*
to pray

here
their place
of worship

giving thanks
to the lord

peace for mankind
health
safety
for their families

I wonder
will they find
an untouched cross
perhaps
a rosary

will they
still
find god

is there
a heaven
amongst such
destruction

perhaps I . . .

I too
should pray

make a space
beneath my knees
lower myself

bow my head

on (beyond the dinosaur)

it is
a skeleton

a ghost
we are leaving behind

people tell
of what it once was

but
all I see
is a dinosaur

bones
and spiking teeth

the spectre
of an
intimidation

that has now
moved on

as we
move on

who knows

did we
do that

did they

I wonder

there's no way
that I know of
to tell

we blew them

then they
blew us

and little blocks
of masonry
hold close
to those secrets

and who
blew what

well
no one is ever
going to know

an entrance (to irony)

there's irony
here
in this bloody war

churches are the first
to go -
in the name
of god -

and people must pray
to remnants
in mortar

here we are
welcomed
by the prison gate

seems *it* could not
be destroyed
no matter
how they tried

a little rest
here
a little repair

then back again

carry the prison
in your mind

your ironic mind

gothically soiled

only the reflection
of the sky
is unstained
here

this
is a gothic
hell

of leaning
and falling

depths
that are entirely
too shallow

without meaning
beyond
crater

beyond
hole

beyond . . .

soiled

stop a minute

well
don't you think
they could
stick-a-sock-in-it
while we're working

trying to get supplies
through a swamp
is not
a joke

as they should know

so wouldn't it be
something
if they held their fire

it's heavy
enough
and its
hard enough
and this swamp
is just crawling
with the once
alive

so I'd appreciate
if they could stop

just
for another
minute

POST CARD
Daily Mail BATTLE PICTURES

These are the men who shortly after midnight of Sunday, July 23, 1916, took Pozières by a splendidly dashing advance through shrapnel, shell, and machine-gun fire.

Official War Photographs.
CROWN COPYRIGHT RESERVED.
Series 5   No 40

Dear Wife,
my wish is that this reached you all in best of health. as it leave myself at present in it indeed of love to you all from yours own
this is fighting order. Best

For Address only

Dear Annie
no 8. Normanby Avenue
Malvern
Melbourne
Victoria
Australia

Printed in England

AWM 90948

and should I fall (then know)

dear wife
I wish that I could tell you
everything

about my thoughts
of you
and my worrying

about you
and about
tomorrow

but it will come
worry
or no

and I will run
I will fight
with you close to me
in my heart

should I fall
then know
I love you
with all I am

stooped (berserk)

I try to keep
my head
low

but
after a while
it doesn't matter

the way I run
now
I'm permanently
stooped

as though
being close to the
ground
might stop
a shell
or a fizzing bullet

and I can't shoot
back
while I'm running

and I will arrive
without
enough air

but adrenaline
and fear
make a berserker
of me

if I should live
they
will surely die

put them right

ah well
it's not just
the younger lads
that want
to see the world

I'm forty-two
after all

and besides
the mother country
is still in peril
and a man needs to do
the right thing

I was just a labourer
back home
so
there was no real
excuse
not to sign up . . .

try to help

my dear lady
was right behind it

you get over there
charlie
and you help them
to put things
right

so yes

see
a bit of the world
and
help put things
right

and it's funny
in a way

I've ended up
still a labourer
only
posted over here now

nearly two weeks
ago

I miss christina
and my old home
in adelaide
a bit
but I'll send a letter
when I get
the chance

and home
will still be there
when I get back
I reckon

once more (the whistle)

well
old black
we have ridden
around them

hallooed
and hurrahed them
from the high country
to the downlands

next time out
it will be
right at their eyes

we will run them
around
and run them right
down

not for us
the green pastures
of the old
riverina

not for us
the high plains
of bogong

it's a slog
in the mud

with not much hoping
for tomorrow
but
if speed counts
and endurance . . .

we'll prevail

old black
my old darling
I'll brush your coat
as I can

to me
you're a beauty
even here

ride

we'll ride
like the devil's
behind us

we'll ride
when the whistles
blow

ride in the dawn
at the sound
of the whistle

pushed (indecently)

you know . . .

the more
I look at
these
poor bastards . . .

wretched creatures

the more
I see myself
reflected

and
there's not so much . . .

not
too much
comfort in that
for me
at all

anyway
come on in back
will you

give the poor beast
a decent push

bray (in the midden)

bray
you ass
go ahead and bray

and swim

swim through the bloody mud
you fool

another day

this is
just
one more
deep-midden day

so bray
all you like
you poor ass

but don't you . . .

don't you *dare*
think
to fall

holes (in the cheese road)

this is a place
of broken
reflections

you can't see
what you were
even just a minute
ago

the cheese road
is filled
with holes

from bombs
that fell
to take away
all our expectations

but
they can't take away
a hope
that no one feels

parched

they want water
near helles

of course
they do

they want water
at ypres

dying
thirsty

and so
we come
through the forest

through the mud

this is water
for the parched

and so
we come

(ever) thirsty

go and fetch
the water
boys

they're thirsty
at the front

almost
as thirsty
as those weeping

in the no man's fields
beyond the trenches
where they cry

thirsty
they will be thirsty

for no man's land
is dry

deserving (better)

on this track
I sent
my burdens

in a carriage
riding high

I sent them
on a journey
with a prayer

I watched them
around
a railway bend

they were almost
out of my sight

when I heard
a shrill
and saw
a flash

I know I said
that they were
burdens

but
even they . . .

even *I* . . .

deserved
so much better

much
better
than that

munition wraiths

shoot . . .

hit . . .

ka boom!

when
a munition
strikes
a munition
well . . .

guy fawkes night
arrives
with extra flare
sometimes

it arrived
in the middle
of july

it arrived
in september

it is here
now

without an effigy
but filled
entire
with wraiths
and spectres

the attractant whistling (the broken)

we stand and watch
for death

coming
perhaps
to us
from bellevarde ridge
or glencourse wood

though
glencourse wood
is nothing now
but
matchsticks impaled
into the mud

this is july . . .

summer
over here
though
you wouldn't know it

the only flowers
are a dance of dust
and mud

that bloom
when the death

that we all await
should fall

maybe
along this track
so rutted . . .

beyond the *corduroy*

a single sign of life
there
would bring the shell

its whistle
and a whiff
that is
the cordite perfumery
of doom
too close

but that point -
on consideration -
should be
a moot one

for the only signs
that are here to see
are lying still
and broken

hunting (in packs) for sanity

we hunt
in packs

we walk
in circles

only the duckboard
keeps us
sane

only the duckboard
keeps our feet
above the mire

and
if only the duckboard
could see
what we have to see
instead of us

and if only
the duckboard
could take us away

from the blood
that soaks
our khaki coats

the guts that we
all carry
as well as lewis guns

we walk
on duckboard
for miles

no sight yet
of sanity

a waddle

they rise
through the smoke

up
into the morning

then
they sit there

watching

sitting ducks
taking photographs

don't they run
like a waddling of pigs
when the fly boys
get after them

don't they just
run

what kind of man
could do that
I wonder

with joes like me
on the ground
ready to take
a pop
at them
with a rifle
if they're not
one of *ours*

what's the weather

rise above the
wreckage

see
what you can see

go high
until the rest of us
are only ants

then
cast your eyes
around
and about

can you see what
and where
they all are

can you tell us
within
a pinpoint

where our batteries
should fire

then hold on . . .

while you're up there
take a look
at where we
strike

tell us if
we scored hits

or
if we missed

and by the way
have you got
blue sky

there's too much
smoke
down here
to tell

tell us
what's the weather like
above ypres

into a duck

it's like
floating
a fish

a big
fat
bloater

but when we get it
up there

it'll change

transmogrify itself
like magic

into a duck

a sitting duck

god bless them
if there's
any fockers
about

flyboys in the wide world

those fly boys

they have
the life

wind whistling
through the struts

them and the clouds
and the whole wide
of the skies

but
my word

don't they just
land
so
very very hard
sometimes

luft (I am not sorry)

luft

is another name
for
in the air

flying free

armed
for observation

but this *luft*-plane
is not
going to see
anything
any more

we have brought
it down
with our bullets

it's a turtle
now
with propeller bust
and broken wings

on its back
forevermore

and I cannot say
that I
am sorry

208

never a horse or a mule (again)

I feed
all these horses

I bleed
for them
as well
yes

for they are
noble

as noble
as anything
I know

but they
and the mules . . .

these poor
bloody
mules

will die
in the mud

just like
the good men
that die
in the same
stinking mud

but
it's horses for me

I have always
held the horse
in my heart

when this
is over

when -
god willing -
I go home

I will never
look
at a horse
no
nor a mule

I will never
look on them
again

no longer for you (the world changes)

from
out of a dream

some kind
of dream

a portent
perhaps
of the end . . .

make way
for the machine

this is no longer
a place
for the likes
of you

make way
for the machine

make way

you might
yet
be the one
who lives

for gingerbread

at a glance
I say
gingerbread

at a glance
I say
gnomes
or dwarves
or ants
all busy-busy

I would not say
soldiers

I would not say
destruction

but this is
no
fairy-tale

no snow white
no
cinderella

just men
who clear the mines

men

who make it
safe
for other men
to blow up
other men

I wish
sometimes for . . .

sometimes
for gingerbread

the baton (my instrument)

I
will pass this baton
on
to you

I will kiss it
goodbye

then throw . . .

will you catch . . .

will it
blow . . .

will you die

I
never knew you

I am just an instrument
played
from afar
by another

perhaps
I do know you

you are just like me
after all

where I stand (is on my knees)

I stand
on
sacred ground

can't you read
the sign

this is no place
for war

this
is *civilised*

and I wonder
if me
standing here
makes me civilised
too

I wonder
if touching the stone
admits me
into the secret

or if that
can only be found
below

among the bones

that will be
soon enough

for me

I can wait
another day

head low

my body
down

upon my
knees

ringing (for our lives)

ring the bell

(*dong*

dong)

to save our lives

ring
the bell
(*dong*)
to save our
very lives

the church
is gone

the bell still rings

when the gas
starts drifting

(*dong*
dong)

the bell will call
to save
our lives

220

a breath (too slow) you die

there is nothing
to see
at hellfire
corner

only a channel
for the guns

ride
and run
from
hellfire corner

if you slow
to take a breath

you'll die

ripple (and wave)

beware
your face
is in the water

that reflection
might be
your fate

beware
you become
your shadow

left to waver
in wriggled lines

that are all
the memory
of you

a shallow ripple
cresting
a receding
wave

still walking

start off
don't look-ing

after a while
it becomes
don't see

there's nothing
here
in the scenery
to keep in mind

so just keep
walking

keep right on
walking

it's nothing like
a sunday stroll
but
at least
you are still
walking

unlike
some poor beggars -

the soldier

the villager

the horse -

lying still
on the road

you can keep
walking

keep *not*
see-ing

and *not smell*-ing

just
ragged-breathing

while you
still walk

glutton

63

The golden sun goes down in peace o'er the desolate wastes of No Man's Land on the Somme.

the golden sun

the sun goes down

the golden
sun

desolation
to its sleeping

the night will come
to take lost souls

away into
safe keeping

no-man
is on the forest steps
spectres dead
still standing . . .

. . . and of the spectres
dead
none standing

blow the bugle
blow it slow

the golden sun
defeated

shining still
but through a cloud

and war is hell

and this
this war
is
hell

oblivion in the smoke

so
we the weary

walk
or ride
or roll

another battle
is waiting

another chance
to live
or die

we move toward
the thicker smoke
as though it holds
a secret
and

so it does

it holds tomorrow

it holds
nothing

somewhere in the smoke
is oblivion

or life

how (here)

I'm pretty sure

if I look at this
the right way

this way
up
or
maybe . . .

maybe
that

yes
yes
maybe up the other way

I'll be able
to see
how the hell
we got into
this
damned mess

AUSTRALIANS PARADING FOR THE TRENCHES. 80

OFFICIAL PHOTOGRAPH.
CROWN COPYRIGHT RESERVED

taking pozieres (a smile for annie)

we are the australian
heroes
of pozieres

hurrah!
hurrah!

hats up
in the air

a smile for annie
and a grin
for mum

hurrah! hurrah!

we will take
pozieres
you know

we will take it
in a splendid
dash

shrapnel -
that's nothing

shellfire -

nothing much

machine guns
can be a problem . . .

but
no
not for us

we
are going to take
pozieres

we will have it
in a rush

even if it
takes
until our last man

our last man
will take
pozieres

even if
it kills him

hurrah!

Waiting to go into action behind the tanks. In that first attack on September 15, 1916, a single tank with two companies of Infantry cleared a mile of trench and, apart from killed and wounded, 370 prisoners were taken with a loss of only five men.

flers (before christmas)

maybe
there'll be
a change

it's hard to think
that might be true

but slowly
some things do change

slowly . . .

we see it
even here

this time
could be the time . . .

could be the place

and maybe
we'll see flers
before christmas

the seer says

well done
boys

so far so good

we're a good platoon
and
we've done all right
so far

but
I can tell you
boys
I've seen the future
and
it doesn't look
too bright

bill and james -

I'm sorry boys

herb and john -
you too

we'll miss your talk
of the smithy
john

we're going to cop
a lot
of flack
fella's

some of us will pass
in the thick
of the action
some by gas
or pneumonia

and a lot
of us
are going to take
wounds

no
don't ask
I won't tell
the rest of you
who gets what

those of us
that are left
will be shuffled
into another battalion

most likely
the 32nd

and I can see
a little bit
further boys

enough to know
this show
will be with us
alive or dead
forever

so
mind how you travel
and now
let's move out

harbonnieres
is ahead of us

to mother (as well)

blow me up
to heaven

I'm coming

blow me
down
to hell

blow my pieces
over the ocean

blow a piece

one piece
home to my mother
as well

battalion blood

weary

we are left
to march

away
from the blood
of our battalion

that will stay to soak
into
these flanders fields

if poppies
rise

let them be
red ones

like our dear (lost) boys

we are ready

ready as
we'll ever be

to run
when the gauntlet's
thrown

one last smoke

a draw
on my trusty
pipe

before the signal

then move out
get amongst
our boys

don't *become*
one of our
dear
lost boys

dog and rabbit

let's see now

let's just
see
if we can get
some of the somme
off this thing

then
we can take
a little look

we'll let the dog
take
a good little look

at his rabbit

I (into the breech)

here
on the street
a glimpse
of hell

here
is my sense
of *no*
sense
confirmed

load up the gun
again

cartridge
into the barrel
by the breech

one
and one . . .

and one . . .

a million
and a half
preliminary
bombs away

. . . and one
and one
and . . .

whistle in the sky

scream
into my ears

. . . one . . .

leave behind
a cemetery lot
made
out of brass

one by one

ten
by ten

a hundred

and *stop*
for I knew them all

and *stop*
I *was* them
all

stop
stop

it is myself
now
into the breech

one final time

without crump

what would it be

what
would a day be
without the crumping noise
and the eternal
rumbling
that I feel
through the soles
of my feet

that I feel
through this cloying
mud
that grips my ankles

what would a day be
without my eardrums
near bursting
and my bowels
turned to water
when the mongrels
whistle down
too close
for my imagination

what would a day be

in turns

puffs of
dust

of mud
really

some poor fool
got his ticket
punched

like as not

them
maybe
and not *us*
this time

look out
get down

it's never too long
before
it's our turn

far and far

how far
is far

not *that* far
not really

not when you can
feel them
through the mud

drilling you down
a little deeper
with every burst

the bastards deserve
their bleeding ears

I hope they don't
hear us coming
when it's our turn

bad luck (for a prayer)

another place
of worship

one more house
of prayer

perhaps
they stand
too tall
these churches

perhaps
the devil
aims the bombs

perhaps it's all
just
bad luck
like the bad luck
that placed anybody
who lived here

within the walls (while we lived)

who lived
inside
these walls

in another time
was it me

that -
what is now
so many
fallen rafters -
was a space
in which
I roamed

a desk
in the corner
was where my son
dreamed himself
into sweet novels

he would write
as long as
there was
paper

above -
there
in the bedroom . . .

I loved my wife
so much
you know

and I wonder
sometimes
if I showed her that
enough
when I
yet could

at the back of the
house
below the collapsed
upper floor

we ate
at one time
around the kitchen
table

and joked
with each other
in a serious way

that only she
and I
ever understood

and food scraps
we saved and gave

chook chook chook

to the fowls
for the eggs
and meat
they gave back
to us

while they lived

while
we lived

when these
were walls
and within
we lived

is not

there is no
hiding
in the forest
of flers

the sticks
that were trees
have no girth
to conceal
even a skinny wretch
like you

and beyond you
and your wretchedness
of trees
I see the village
that once
was

and now
is not

is not

anymore

Lille, 1916.

residence (lost)

oh
my sweet city
what have they done
to you

nothing stands
where once
my heart
was a resident

more
than I knew

I was yours
was
of you

where

where
is my heart
now
to live

gone (before I sleep)

and this
once
my home

that wall

it held
a crucifix
to bless the house -
my house

the picture
of my wife
the day we wed

now
it covers all -
like soil
spread across an open
grave -
that was
all
of my life

the whole of me

what now
for
such as me

this is the village
of all my fathers

is the place
I reared
my sons

both gone
now
taken by a day
already
completely forgotten

I have no
village
left to me

I have no life

no
not even my mules
nor horses

all gone
and blown
to hell

as I
will likely die

blown to hell

alone
and left
to a falling shell

long hours

long hours
before I sleep

silent striking

and where
did all of albert
go

I have looked
but all I see
are cavities
and spaces

outlines of -
once -
a town

the silence
here is broken
only
by the soft nicker
of my horse
and the sound
of a single match
striking

420

glutton

I live
in a hole
in the ground

I share it
with a rat
and some lice
that think they own me

we have reached
an agreement
a compromise
about the food

I eat
from soggy ration packs
the lice
eat
from me

the rat
will not discuss
his cuisine
or culinary treasures

but I talk to him -
so sleek -

I tell him
not to eat
too much
of my ex-comrades

better
to go find
the enemy
though
I think he finds it
hard to choose
between the who and the
who

water
in the trenches

I lost a toe
last winter

cold and hot
and ice
and water

thank god
the rains let up
thank god
they still send us
cigarettes
from time to time

sometimes I feel
I can hide myself
inside a twirling column
of the grey that flows
when I light up

I could just
disappear

I don't
really
live in this
hole in the ground
where you've found me

I'm only temporary -
passing through -
resident
for just a short while

my home
is somewhere
further
a small away off
in the trenches

among the crater holes
of mud and blood
left behind
by falling shells
one day
they will bury
my lice and me
(whether I am dead
or not)

did I happen to mention
my rat

he will remain
when I must leave

good luck to him
and may he die
a glutton

certainly
I hope he dies

a glutton

where we breathe (underground)

we are all the same

I
over here
and you . . .

at least for you
all fighting's done

at least
for you a place
to lie in peace

while I have to catch
my breath

a paltry breath
before the whistle
blows again

you and I
inhale the same -
this musty stuff -
my friend

our air is one
shared
inspiration

breathed underground

digging (for victory)

dig in
boys

I think
we must have
won

dig in . . .
I am weary
to the bone

boys
we are not what
we used to be

so many
in shallow graves

we are not
what we were
when we left
victoria

we are not
what we were
just yesterday

mouquet farm
and that damned
pozieres
have done for us

for what we were

so dig in
boys
keep digging
in

this ground
is ours

god knows
it cost
enough

again (tomorrow)

what have you
got
growing
on your feet today
lads

let's have a quick
butchers
at them . . .

what have you got
today

anyone
with a bit
of itching

anyone
losing skin

anybody
got a touch
of trench-foot

that could win
a holiday
for the lucky one

so bring them
out

bring them
out
and I will
take a look

a daily
little look . . .

no
sorry boys
you look all right

I'll have another
sticky-beak
tomorrow

you can't tell them (back home)

would you like
a drink
cobber

I'll just step
across
to the water tank

there's
plenty there

if you can wait . . .

it's a little cold
cobber

you don't see
winters
like this
at home

I don't know
how to write it
down

so my mum
might understand

fancy
ice on your eyebrows

fancy freezing
your exhaled
breath

and fancy
icing up
while you're trying
to have a pee

you can't write that
for them
back home

you just can't say that
to them
back at home

the weight of fireworks

come on
you men

let's haul this mud
and the damned
eighteen pounder
inside it

it's a lazy
machine
only fit
to spit lead

and it won't
move itself
from the mire

if we want
fireworks
tonight
pull your weight

pull your weight

you better

pull your weight

how do I know (unknow)

how do I cross
this bog

how do I know
where to place
each footstep

my comrades lie

my comrades lie

how do I cross
this bog
of graves

I cannot see them

I cannot know
until . . .

I cannot
un-know
ever again

not ever
again

ever (real)

now

there are none

who knew
who didn't know

who should
have known

there are
none

and there is no fricourt
no manor
no farmhouse
no animals
no crop

and all of us
are dead

haunting craters

and wondering
if 1913
was ever real

if this nightmare
of *now*
is ever
real

an eye on the diamantina

I signed up
because
my mates and me
had never seen rain
out
on the diamantina

all we'd ever done
was push
cattle
from the back
of a horse

and back
in mother england
they were asking
for help

so
a little bit
of sailing the ocean
wasn't bad

and
a bit of fighting
johnny turkey
on gallipoli
wasn't bad

but I've ended up here
in the stinking slop
with just one
eye

and my mates
are all dead

shot to hell
in pieces

so I promenade
the mud fields

like a sentry
on perimeter patrol

the one
I've got left
is enough to see
that we were
foolish

and now I wish
that I
was on the back
of my horse

in front of me
the cattle
would be slowly
moving

and I wish with all my
heart
to see
again
the dry
of the diamantina

wholesome

and we bring you
our darling girls
to these hot
sands

and
strange places

good morning

enjoy your breakfast

this may be
the last
whole

the last
wholesome

for a while

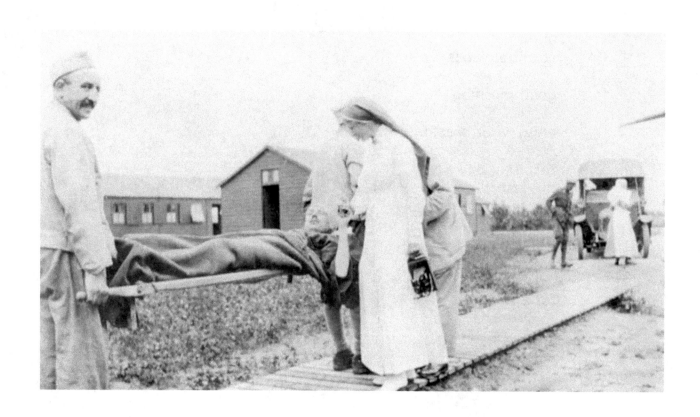

fields (of bluebirds)

florence herself
went
to the blood fields
of the crimea

and who are we
as nurses
not to try
to help
those poor dear boys
who every day
lie bleeding
with only the blackness
and bleakness
to play before their
eyes

let the veil
on our heads
mark us
as bluebirds

let the veil
that they see
mark *us* as
life

or
at least
as an idea
of grace
in these wretched fields
of suffering
and mud

and
of dying

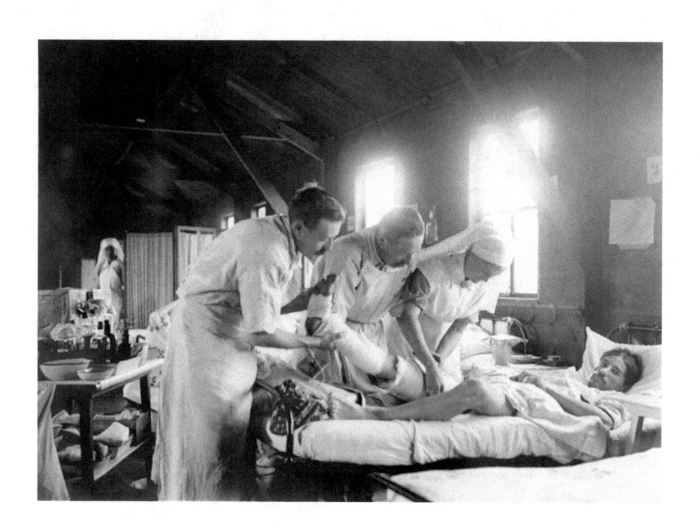

the devil (to heal)

easy now

keep it still
for me
gentlemen

these holes
are big enough that
back home
we'd ask the local council
to fill them
with road base

at least
we still have
bandages

and at least
there seems
some chance
that this might heal

gangrene
is the very devil

let us see

aye lads
we have come

strong arms
will carry you

trucks
and wagons
await

bullets
and shrapnel

the stuff
of all our lives

hold on
lads

let us see
if we can
save you

moments to wonder what

all our lives -
taken together -
were meant
to mean
something

here
on a stretcher
laid down
in the calcifying mud

I am not so certain
anymore
that I know
where the meaning
resides

I thought once
of glory

I was filled
with the idea
and with pride

but I've seen
that the passing
of my best mate
was nothing . . .

meant nothing

a small pool
of blood

a last gasp
of air

my enemy
will carry me

we will both
be glad
we are out

away
from it

he is just
a man
in the end

and I
have had moments
to wonder

just what am I

ah well

on menin mud

shot my mouth
off

shot my arm

we walk
in numbers
so we can find
the road

lay us down
on stretchers
if we
cannot stand

we
cannot walk

when they blow apart
our ambulance
they
let us
float

high
on menin mud

not dead (enough)

look at it

the bastards
won't give us
a minute's peace

even after
they've done us
in

they've got to go
out of their way
to kill us
again

bastards

302

too many everywhere we go

too many
crosses

we leave them
everywhere

oh
do you know
where
the australians
have been

    yes yes

    it is a cemetery
    now

    yes yes

    that
    is where
    they've been

but
what are we
to do

we leave
a part of us

the best part
of us

too many
crosses
everywhere we go

but that
is where
we've been

laying in arms

thank god
for pozieres
where we can
bury
our dead

because
there is not
enough room
in australia

to lay them all
down

comrades

dear comrades
in arms

no surprises

sometimes
I wonder
while I'm looking
for a mate

if what I find
might be
myself . . .

how would I know

if this is
existence
or
if it's hell

hell on earth
with an open mouth
to eat us all

yeah
it wouldn't
surprise me
if it was *myself*
that I'm looking for

wouldn't surprise
if I found
me
either

no
no surprise

not
at all

what and who (we breathe)

this dust we breathe
was last month's
mud

in which we fought

in which
we died

now
it fills the air
as boot
and tyre
and wagon
pass

I wonder
what

I wonder
who

this air is
thick
with us

and yet we must
go on
and breathe it

310

seeing us in (final) trenches

and sometimes . . .

sometimes I see them
all
at once

every one of them
running
in heavy boots
to meet
their own
dying

falling down
before they have even
risen
from these
wretched
wretched
trenches

holes
we call our home

that accommodate
our doom

that keep us
barely alive
while we
are waiting

the whistle to blow

all of us
and all at once
and up we go
and down we fall

I see them

I see myself

all of us
in our trenches

weary of

it is a
procession
of the mourning

I hear the songs
they sing
for the dead

they were
many

they are few

they are weary
hauling
these engines
and machines

until their song
is another word
of dying

let the guns
sound

a barrage
once again

let the shells
fly
whistling
above them

let the boom
sound out
in a cry
to the god of war

these men
and their machines
are weary
from carrying their
dead

and of
the dying

314

knackered

perhaps
he has the secret

perhaps
he's defusing
a bomb

more likely
he's looking for a deck
of playing cards

whatever

he's got it
on his own

I'm not helping
and
if he blows us all up

well
bugger him
he can shout the beer
on the other side

I'm too damn knackered
to care
and today -
tonight -
I'm going to be
sleeping

ride of the fallen

and the fallen
slowly
ride

their steeds
point
to valhalla

once proud
and upright
they slump now
in their saddles

they are surely dead
even if
alive

at least
on this ride
there are tall trees
and shade

at least
this time
is safe

and see
they keep coming

their parade
runs
forever

is there room
enough
do you think

will heaven hold
them all

no bombs
no bullets

no shells
from above

let none disturb
the bugle
as it calls

ironic rail

can we build
a railway
to get us
out
of here

I'm laying track
as though
we can

and the engine
of our escape
is keeping pace

it will arrive
just after
we do

irony
is something
that we live with
every day

perhaps to home

on a duckboard highway
we are
bringing the wounded
home

away from the blast
of sound
and the grasping mud

from nowhere . . .

. . . to nowhere

but
somewhere ahead
is where
we're going

somewhere
on a duckboard highway
is safety

perhaps
home

almost (not quite)

it could almost
be
old times

home times

it could
almost
be normal
this gathering of men
at the end
of a day
digging ditches
shoring up walls
and ceilings

enjoying
a cup of tea

a cigarette

and a game of cards
by candlelight

almost

not quite

the few (march)

the march
of the lucky

few
we are

the march of the lucky
few

we march
on a lucky
road
we few
we march

underneath the lucky
leaves

for this road
is out of reach
and we few
are out of reach

and the ghosts
of our comrades
march with us

they march
with the lucky
few

leaving (the somme) now

get
on board
we're tomorrow
bound

get on board
hear
the whistle blow

a ghostly
train
taking passengers
now

get on board
we're tomorrow
bound

don't need
a ticket

there's no need
to pay

this train
will leave
when you take
your place

so rise
like mist
fine
from your deep
shell hole

this train will leave

come on
away

> *<a brief interlude
> of whistling>*

get on board now
(like mist
like smoke)
come on
and get away

to see such heroes

who would have thought
the day
could produce

such a sight
as this

conquering heroes
brought
so low

fluctuation
on fluctuation

.

.

.

that I should have lived
so long

.

.

.

to see this

over

after
the gas
you gifted
has long blown away

after
the mines
I
left for you

after all the bullets
have flown

your brother
and my brother
laid down
together

here we are

our battles all . . .

well

this battle (at least)
over

332

survived

well done
aubrey
you survived

gallipoli

the western front

distinguished conduct

and illness
and debility

but survival
is
survival
all the same

at twenty-eight
enlisted

at thirty-two
home
with a wife

three children

and then . . .

and then

buried
at fifty

too young but
aubrey
you survived

taking all

this cemetery
is the war

it goes on
and on

just keeps going

men like me
get eaten
consumed
by the one

then
held close
by the other

on and on

it won't end
no
not until -
between them -
they have taken us
all

this field (the river)

this field
is a river

I see my face
reflected
in her waters

~

this field
it is a river

I feel her waters
rippling
across my face

~

this field
that is the river

I feel her
carry me

carry me away
towards
the wide sea

~

this field

touch a place (on the avenue)

and I watch
your tree
grow

old

as you
did not

young man

boy volunteer

that was a time
that ate
its own children

I touch the roughness
of the bark
gracing the avenue

touch the roughness
of places
that you fought

touch the place
that you
died

Image Sources

welcome, welcome

for glory

> 12th Battalion of Australian Infantry Forces marching through Hobart, Tasmania
>
> https://www.flickr.com/photos/hwmobs/9757832354

to remember (we will play)

> 30th Battalion. Entering Kiama Station. August 1916.
>
> https://www.flickr.com/photos/25022128@N03/9097898318
>
> Kiama Library collection.

going somewhere

> On the Way', France
>
> https://collections.museumvictoria.com.au/items/1700751
>
> Sergeant John Lord, 1916 in Museums Victoria Collections

for pride

> Private Malcolm Mcintosh Southwell, 20th Battalion AIF, who was killed in action on The Somme, France, On 1916-11-15
>
> https://www.awm.gov.au/collection/C40733
>
> AWM Accession Number P00124.001

and serious (for mum)

> Three Australian Soldiers portrait
>
> https://trove.nla.gov.au/work/234865916
>
> Aussie~mobs (2019). Three Australian soldiers in France - WW1. Image Number 45730450795

the strolling women (of Pont d'Achelles)

> A group of women, Pont d'Achelles
>
> https://collections.museumvictoria.com.au/items/1700727
>
> Sergeant John Lord, 1916 in Museums Victoria Collections

unease (until they go)

    Man Near Property Gate, Ergnies

    https://collections.museumvictoria.com.au/items/1954899

    Sergeant John Lord, 1916 in Museums Victoria Collections

hurry (they come)

    Horse drawn carts in a French village

    https://collections.museumvictoria.com.au/items/1703067

    Sergeant John Lord, 1916 in Museums Victoria Collections

sister (photograph)

    Australian soldiers with a French girl

    https://collections.museumvictoria.com.au/items/1703746

    Sergeant John Lord, 1916 in Museums Victoria Collections

for a romp

    Light horseman, Egypt 1916

    https://digital.slq.qld.gov.au/delivery/DeliveryManagerServlet?change_lng=en&dps_pid=IE1024677

    Burdekin Shire Council Library Services

(so very) old and (so very) young

    a French farm wagon

    https://collections.museumvictoria.com.au/items/1703073

    Sergeant John Lord, 1916 in Museums Victoria Collections

making a home

    A dugout with its entrance protected by sandbags. A spade rests on top of the dugout at left.

    https://www.awm.gov.au/collection/C274039

    AWM Accession Number P01835.065

and a spade

    A view of the Flers Battlefield, showing an old front line trench improved by the Australians

    https://www.awm.gov.au/collection/C43222

    AWM Accession Number E00519 - Imisson, Horace B

pay you (a winkle)

> An Australian buying winkles (molluscs) from a French hawker in a village on the Somme
>
> https://www.awm.gov.au/collection/C54478
>
> AWM Accession Number E00048

soon (would you like a cup of tea?)

> Y.M.C.A. Dug-out in Rossignol Wood, at the Somme, FranceWW1
>
> https://trove.nla.gov.au/work/235436779
>
> Aussie~mobs (2019). Y.M.C.A. Dug-out in Rossignol Wood, at the Somme, France - WW1. Image Number 47439887821

the best day

> An Australian motor cyclist cleaning the mud from his machine
>
> https://www.awm.gov.au/collection/C389098
>
> AWM Accession Number E00047

pretty place

> A general view of the city of Albert
>
> https://www.awm.gov.au/collection/C1024
>
> AWM Accession Number C04922

who could imagine (in 1913)

> Local men standing on rail tracks in front of the railway station at Fricourt c. 1913
>
> https://www.awm.gov.au/collection/C1013308
>
> AWM Accession Number C03133

easier (should be)

> 'Marseilles Entraining', Francez
>
> https://collections.museumvictoria.com.au/items/1700749
>
> Sergeant John Lord, 1916 in Museums Victoria Collections

ok (we were)

> Studio portrait of 2158 private James Mccrae Hancock, 23rd Battalion, who was killed in action at Pozieres
>
> https://www.awm.gov.au/collection/C41543
>
> AWM Accession Number P00163.001

one cuppa (a week)

'Pea Soup or Cocoa', Longueval, France

https://collections.museumsvictoria.com.au/items/2010157

Museums Victoria Collections

marching (closer)

'Armentieres Road', France

https://collections.museumvictoria.com.au/items/1700728

Sergeant John Lord, 1916 in Museums Victoria Collections

captured (in a photograph)

Farmhouse, Lake & Horses, Neuf Berquin, France

https://collections.museumvictoria.com.au/items/1700744

Sergeant John Lord, 1916 in Museums Victoria Collections

safe (until)

'Wardrecques', France

https://collections.museumvictoria.com.au/items/1700742

Sergeant John Lord, 1916 in Museums Victoria Collections

every breath a hope

Germany, c. 1916. portrait of two German children aged about six and four.

https://www.awm.gov.au/collection/C206934

AWM Accession Number P00167.002

we'll send him clean

Burial Party, Neuf Berquin, France

https://collections.museumvictoria.com.au/items/1700745

Sergeant John Lord, 1916 in Museums Victoria Collections

lost (as I am)

Studio portrait of 4802 Private John James White, 22nd Battalion, with his wife Lillian, son Colin and baby daughter Myrl.

https://www.awm.gov.au/collection/C1103696

AWM Accession Number DA14919A

sheep on the somme

> Group portrait of four unidentified soldiers wearing sheepskin vests to ward off the cold.
>
> https://www.awm.gov.au/collection/C1294154
>
> AWM Accession Number P10550.158

pausing (while I rest)

> Australian troops amidst the devastation of war. A scene at Ypres, ca. 1917
>
> http://hdl.handle.net/10462/deriv/2063
>
> State Library of Queensland. Negative Number: 194858

this war (by bike)

> On a child's bike
>
> https://www.awm.gov.au/collection/A00815
>
> AWM Accession Number A00815

winner

> A group of unidentified Australians behind the ruins of Ypres, playing their popular game of 'two up'.
>
> https://www.awm.gov.au/collection/C54955
>
> AWM Accession Number E01199

pudding on Christmas

> The interior of the British Expeditionary Force (BEF) Canteen just before Christmas 1916.
>
> https://www.awm.gov.au/collection/C54489
>
> AWM Accession Number E00101

damper and

> Cooks of the 58th Battalion with their field cooker (mobile kitchen) at Dickebusch, near Ypres, where the 5th Australian Division rested after the Third Battle of Ypres.
>
> https://www.awm.gov.au/collection/C1110
>
> AWM Accession Number E01100

jalopied heart

> Motor and horse transport passing through Vlamertinghe, near Ypres.
>
> https://www.awm.gov.au/collection/C43224
>
> AWM Accession Number E00872 - Hurley, James Francis (Frank), 1917

lost robbie

A portrait of 918 Private Robert Wilson, 34th Battalion. Private Wilson was killed in the battle of Passchendaele on 1917-10-13.

https://www.awm.gov.au/collection/C281435

AWM Accession Number P01920.005

when we met (on herberg street)

Busses conveying the 2nd Division to the Ypres sector passing through the town, along Herberg Street. Frank Hurley, 1917

https://www.awm.gov.au/collection/C392593

AWM Accession Number E02012 - Hurley, James Francis (Frank), 1917

one to take care (of his grieving mother)

A portrait of 1477 Private James Barker, 34th Battalion Born Jan 1863, Died 20 Jul 1917.

https://www.awm.gov.au/collection/C281442

AWM Accession Number P01920.012

one to take care (of his grieving mother)

A portrait of 2534 Private John Albert Barker, 35th Battalion. Private Barker died on 191`7-06-7.

https://www.awm.gov.au/collection/C281446

AWM Accession Number P01920.016

welcome (welcome)

Devastated landscape of the Ypres sector, Flanders, 1917 Frank Hurley

https://nla.gov.au/nla.obj-158877388

Hurley, Frank. Devastated landscape of the Ypres sector, Flanders, 1917

a swamp (of all the world)

commanders? I do not think so

France. c. 1916-08. Marshal J.J.C. Joffre, on the left, French Army Commander, Sir Douglas Haig

https://www.awm.gov.au/collection/C309971

AWM Accession Number H08416

a corpse: a crop

> Mouquet Farm before destruction
>
> https://www.awm.gov.au/collection/C1717
>
> AWM Accession Number Accession Number J00181

come the morning

> 'Shattered Remains of Mouquet Farm', France, World War I, Oct 1916
>
> https://collections.museumvictoria.com.au/articles/14946
>
> Buchan, N. (2016) The Battle of the Somme, 1916 in Museums Victoria Collections

mountains until

> Mouquet Farm
>
> https://www.awm.gov.au/collection/E00998
>
> AWM Accession Number E00998

mountains until

> Mouquet Farm
>
> https://www.awm.gov.au/collection/C377073
>
> AWM Accession Number H15927

trenchant plans

> German soldier in a communication trench leading to Pozieres
>
> https://www.awm.gov.au/collection/C60187
>
> AWM Accession Number J00218

poor ivor (1)

> Ivor Margetts
>
> https://www.awm.gov.au/collection/C374681
>
> AWM Accession Number C374681

run (fortified)

> Over the top, amid bursting gas and tear shells, in a determined assault on the fortified Somme villages
>
> https://repository.monash.edu/items/show/25821
>
> Realistic Travels Company, "Over the top, amid bursting gas and tear shells, in a determined assault on the fortified Somme villagers,"

no time (giddap)

    Ambulances on the Road to Wardrecques

    https://collections.museumvictoria.com.au/items/1700741

    Sergeant John Lord, 1916 in Museums Victoria Collections

clip clop (stay alive)

    The road at La Boiselle

    https://collections.museumvictoria.com.au/items/1703711

    Sergeant John Lord, 1916 in Museums Victoria Collections

500 yards (north of montauban) (mon-tar-ben)

    Tent Where Shapley was Killed, Somme, France, Sergeant John Lord, World War I, 1916

    https://collections.museumsvictoria.com.au/items/1706344

    Sergeant John Lord, 1916 in Museums Victoria Collections

two pennies up (for the ambulance)

    Grave of Private H.G. Shapley, Somme, France, Sergeant John Lord, World War I, 1916

    https://collections.museumsvictoria.com.au/items/1706342

    Sergeant John Lord, 1916 in Museums Victoria Collections

two pennies up (for the ambulance)

    Grave of Private H.G. Shapley, Somme, France, Sergeant John Lord, World War I, 1916

    https://collections.museumsvictoria.com.au/items/1706345

    Sergeant John Lord, 1916 in Museums Victoria Collections

not west australia

    Staff Sergeant Kemp, Somme, France

    https://collections.museumvictoria.com.au/items/1706323

    Sergeant John Lord, 1916 in Museums Victoria Collections

poor ivor (2)

    Ivor Margetts lonely Grave

    https://www.awm.gov.au/collection/E00532

    AWM Accession Number E00532

the un-pock game (let's bomb ypres)

> Aerial view of the line from which the 3rd Battle of Ypres started.
>
> https://www.awm.gov.au/collection/C1754
>
> AWM Accession Number J00274

staccato

> Somme Area, France. 1916-06-29. French artillerymen working on a 400mm gun at Ravin d'Harbonnieres
>
> https://www.awm.gov.au/collection/C297095
>
> AWM Accession Number H04510

hush

> Somme Area, France. 1916-06-29. A camouflaged French 400mm gun at Ravin d'Harbonnieres.
>
> https://www.awm.gov.au/collection/C297093
>
> AWM Accession Number H04508

rabbit hole

> a part of the Australian front line at Gueudecourt, showing sandbag reinforcement, duckboards and timber bridge over water-filled shell hole.
>
> https://www.awm.gov.au/collection/C41252
>
> AWM Accession Number P00308.006

another night (like this)

> The bombardment of Beaumont Hamel 2 July 1916
>
> https://collection.nam.ac.uk/detail.php?acc=1995-03-86-15
>
> NAM 1995-03-86-15

wondering (and bullets)

> Hun Dugout with elaborate fittings
>
> https://collections.museumvictoria.com.au/items/1703729
>
> Sergeant John Lord, 1916 in Museums Victoria Collections

once (like lightning)

> Six inch gun flash at night (Christmas Eve, 1916)
>
> https://collections.museumvictoria.com.au/items/1706324
>
> Sergeant John Lord, 1916 in Museums Victoria Collections

would the guns might kiss

> Havoc caused by German guns near Bapaume
>
> https://www.awm.gov.au/collection/C41254
>
> AWM Accession Number P00308.008

duck (the winter mud)

> A light railway train loaded with duckboards
>
> https://www.awm.gov.au/collection/C54916
>
> AWM Accession Number E00816

marching gear

> Laying Duckboard Track, Ypres, Belgium, World War I, 1917
>
> https://collections.museumvictoria.com.au/items/1782447
>
> Museums Victoria Collections

hidden (by smoke)

> A fatigue party of three unidentified soldiers carrying duckboards along a duckboard pathway MolenhoekBecelaereYpres.
>
> https://www.awm.gov.au/collection/C53489
>
> AWM Accession Number A00007 - Gornall, William Arthur

with a duckboard

> The Great War. Reconstructing a bridge over The Somme near Peronne:
>
> http://handle.slv.vic.gov.au/10381/321101
>
> Rose, George, 1861-1942, photographer, State Library of Victoria catalogue: pi006555

a swamp (of all the world)

> Five Australians, members of a field artillery brigade, passing along a duckboard track over mud
>
> https://www.awm.gov.au/collection/C1119
>
> AWM Accession Number E01220

hit the plume

> Near North Chimney, Albert
>
> https://collections.museumvictoria.com.au/items/1703714
>
> Sergeant John Lord, 1916 in Museums Victoria Collections

a bullseye of boredom

> German shells bursting on a wrecked building in the town.
>
> https://www.awm.gov.au/collection/C303357
>
> AWM Accession Number H04280

of what was

> Australian infantry watching the artillery bombardment of Pozieres.
>
> https://www.awm.gov.au/collection/C194642
>
> AWM Accession Number EZ0083

rolling (bread and wine)

> View of the Amiens battlefield with a tracked supply vehicle travelling along a road.
>
> https://www.awm.gov.au/collection/C43279
>
> AWM Accession Number E03924

an orchard (full of apples)

> Two men of the 7th Australian Light Trench Mortar Battery operate a light trench mortar
>
> https://www.awm.gov.au/collection/C1244
>
> AWM Accession Number E02677

a dolour a day

> British Army stretcher bearers moving forward to bring back soldiers wounded near Ginchy
>
> https://www.awm.gov.au/collection/C310397
>
> AWM Accession Number H08451

(ghost of) a chance

> Destroyed shell of a German Ambulance
>
> https://collections.museumvictoria.com.au/items/1703698
>
> Sergeant John Lord, 1916 in Museums Victoria Collections

should I fall

home abandoned (spirit gone)

> Destroyed Building, Somme, France
>
> https://collections.museumvictoria.com.au/items/1759790
>
> Newspaper Illustrations Ltd, 161A Strand, Westminster, Greater London, England, Great Britain

sweet mary (come straight down)

    'Basilica of Notre-Dame de Berbers', Albert, France,

    https://collections.museumvictoria.com.au/items/1703721

    Sergeant John Lord, 1916 in Museums Victoria Collections

cathedral (my heart)

    Neuve Eglise', Belgium

    https://collections.museumvictoria.com.au/items/1700719

    Sergeant John Lord, 1916 in Museums Victoria Collections

bow my head

    The Road to The Church

    https://collections.museumvictoria.com.au/items/1759718

    Newspaper Illustrations Ltd, 161A Strand, Westminster, Greater London, England, Great Britain

on (beyond the dinosaur)

    Ypres Sector, Belgium. 25 October 1917. Australians on the way to take up a front line position in the Ypres Sector.

    https://www.awm.gov.au/collection/C1351

    AWM Accession Number E04612

who knows

    An unidentified Australian in the right foreground surveying the bombed building in the ruined city of Ypres.

    https://www.awm.gov.au/collection/C952033

    AWM Accession Number E00719 - Hurley, James Francis (Frank), 1917

an entrance (to irony)

    The entrance to the prison at Ypres, which was used as a forward dressing station by the 9th Australian Field Ambulance during the Third Battle of Ypres.

    https://www.awm.gov.au/collection/C1015610

    AWM Accession Number C04577

gothically soiled

    'A Big Crater', Ypres, Belgium, World War I, 25 Sep 1917

    https://collections.museumvictoria.com.au/items/2102772

    Museums Victoria Collections

stop a minute

Under great difficulties our troops carry supplies over destroyed bridges on the Ypres Canal

https://repository.monash.edu/items/show/25857

Realistic Travels Company, "Under great difficulties our troops carry supplies over destroyed bridges on the Ypres Canal," Monash Collections Online.

and should I fall (then know)

Postcard: Private Albert Edward Kemp to Annie Kemp, 'Australians Parading for the Trenches', circa 1916

https://collections.museumvictoria.com.au/items/1243799

Museums Victoria Collections

stooped (berserk)

Ginchy, France. September 1916. British Army troops advancing to attack enemy positions

https://www.awm.gov.au/collection/C325506

AWM Accession Number H12254

put them right

The grave of 6042 Private (Pte) Charles Buckley, 27th Battalion, in the Noreuil Australian Cemetery.

https://www.awm.gov.au/collection/C1698

AWM Accession Number J00064

once more (the whistle)

the horse

https://collections.museumvictoria.com.au/items/1954791

Sergeant John Lord, 1916 in Museums Victoria Collections

pushed (indecently)

A mule team bogged in the mud near Potijze Farm, Ypres

https://stors.tas.gov.au/AI/CRO3-1-17

(1917). Photograph - A mule team bogged in the mud near Potijze Farm, Ypres. Libraries Tasmania

bray (into the midden)

A typical illustration of the difficulties encountered in the Ypres Sector

https://www.awm.gov.au/collection/E00963

AWM Accession Number E00963

holes (in the cheese road)

> Unidentified soldiers, probably of the 12th Brigade, moving along a support line known as 'Cheese Road'.
>
> https://www.awm.gov.au/collection/C43120
>
> AWM Accession Number E00576

parched

> Water carriers of the 45th Battalion near the Helles pillbox, moving up towards Molenaarelsthoek, in the Ypres salient.
>
> https://www.awm.gov.au/collection/C336368
>
> AWM Accession Number E00770

(ever) thirsty

> A water carrying fatigue party of the 1st Division passing through the Menin Gate of Ypres, after having delivered a water ration to the front line troops.
>
> https://www.awm.gov.au/collection/C382407
>
> AWM Accession Number E04678

deserving (better)

> Three rail trucks that ploughed off the tracks near Ypres when struck by shells.
>
> https://www.awm.gov.au/collection/C1001628
>
> AWM Accession Number C01355

munition wraiths

> The remains of an exploded ammunition train at Birr Cross Roads in the Ypres Sector. The explosion was the result of a direct hit.
>
> https://www.awm.gov.au/collection/C55080
>
> AWM Accession Number E04675

the attractant whistling (the broken)

> 'The Corduroy Track', Westheok Ridge to Bellevarde, Ypres, Belgium, 26 Oct 1917
>
> https://www.awm.gov.au/collection/C955939
>
> AWM Accession Number E01318

hunting (in packs) for sanity

> A Lewis gun team on a duckboard track near Lake Farm, in the Ypres Sector.
>
> https://www.awm.gov.au/collection/C54940
>
> AWM Accession Number E01087

a waddle

> Observation Balloons
>
> https://collections.museumvictoria.com.au/items/1706365
>
> Sergeant John Lord, 1916 in Museums Victoria Collections

a waddle

> Observation Balloons
>
> https://collections.museumvictoria.com.au/items/1706366
>
> Sergeant John Lord, 1916 in Museums Victoria Collections

what's the weather

> An observation balloon ready to ascend over Ypres.
>
> https://www.awm.gov.au/collection/C46052
>
> AWM Accession Number E01254

into a duck

> A large group of unidentified soldiers inflating an observation balloon near Ypres.
>
> https://www.awm.gov.au/collection/C46051
>
> AWM Accession Number E01248 - Hurley, James Francis (Frank), 1917

flyboys in the wide world

> A British FE2 Pusher aircraft which crashed near the Ypres-Poperinghe Road on 1 November.
>
> https://www.awm.gov.au/collection/C52217
>
> AWM Accession Number E04616

luft (I am not sorry)

> A German L.V.G. C.V aircraft brought down by Australian machine gun fire, at Aeroplane Farm, in the Ypres Sector.
>
> https://www.awm.gov.au/collection/C1102
>
> AWM Accession Number E00897

never a horse or a mule (again)

> Horses Feeding at Allied Camp, Strazeele, France
>
> https://collections.museumvictoria.com.au/items/1700756
>
> Sergeant John Lord, 1916 in Museums Victoria Collections

no longer for you (the world changes)

> Tank
>
> https://collections.museumvictoria.com.au/items/1703723
>
> Sergeant John Lord, 1916 in Museums Victoria Collections

no longer for you (the world changes)

> Tank (a)
>
> https://collections.museumvictoria.com.au/items/1706313
>
> Sergeant John Lord, 1916 in Museums Victoria Collections

for gingerbread

> The ruins of Swan Chateau, in the Ypres Sector, when the 2nd Australian Pioneers were billeted there.
>
> https://www.awm.gov.au/collection/C1324
>
> AWM Accession Number E03870

the baton (my instrument)

> Two German soldiers with hand grenades ready in a trench on Hill 60.
>
> https://www.awm.gov.au/collection/C193816
>
> AWM Accession Number H12366

where I stand (is on my knees)

> Notice on the ruins of Ypres Cathedral: "This is holy ground"
>
> https://www.awm.gov.au/collection/C45188
>
> AWM Accession Number P00735.019 - Holmes, Leonard Malcolm

ringing (for our lives)

> View of a church bell erected on the ramparts of Ypres, and used as a gas alarm.
>
> https://www.awm.gov.au/collection/C954553
>
> AWM Accession Number E01058

a breath (too slow) you die

> Hellfire Corner on the Menin Road, in the Ypres sector in Belgium, on September 27th, 1917.
>
> http://handle.slv.vic.gov.au/10381/230266
>
> Wilkins, G., Captain, photographer (attributed) 1917

ripple (and wave)

> German Army soldiers in a shell cratered area near the town in the Ypres salient.

> https://www.awm.gov.au/collection/H13356

> AWM Accession Number H13356 - Deutsche Reichsarchiv

still walking

> A Scene on the Road Near Ypres', World War I, Ypres, Belgium, 14 Sep 1917

> https://www.awm.gov.au/collection/C1253126

> AWM Accession Number P09114.023 - Hurley, James Francis (Frank), 1917

glutton

the golden sun

> The golden sun goes down in peace o'er the desolate wastes of No Man's Land on the Somme

> https://repository.monash.edu/items/show/25827

> Realistic Travels Company, "The golden sun goes down in peace o'er the desolate wastes of No Man's Land on the Somme," Monash Collections Online.

oblivion in the smoke

> On the way to the line

> https://collections.museumvictoria.com.au/items/1703742

> Sergeant John Lord, 1916 in Museums Victoria Collections

how (here)

> A member of the 1st Machine Gun Battalion maps out trenches near Ypres.

> https://www.awm.gov.au/collection/C387964

> AWM Accession Number P03137.006

taking pozieres (a smile for annie)

> Postcard: Australian Servicemen Before Battle of Pozieres

> https://collections.museumvictoria.com.au/items/391053

> Museums Victoria Collections

flers (before christmas)

> Group of Infantrymen & Mk I Tank, Battle of Flers-Courcelette

> https://collections.museumsvictoria.com.au/items/394931

> Museums Victoria Collections

the seer says

> Lieutenant Rupert Frederick Arding Downes MC addressing his Platoon from B Company, 29th Battalion.
>
> https://www.awm.gov.au/collection/C1251
>
> AWM Accession Number E02790

to mother (as well)

> At Hellfire Corner on the Menin Road, during the Third Battle of Ypres
>
> http://nla.gov.au/nla.obj-159896563
>
> Hurley, Frank. (1914). [At Hellfire Corner on the Menin Road, during the Third Battle of Ypres, World War I]

battalion blood

> A scene along the Ypres Road, showing a tired Battalion coming out to rest.
>
> https://www.awm.gov.au/collection/C953165
>
> AWM Accession Number E00843 - Hurley, James Francis (Frank), 1917

like our dear (lost) boys

> Ambulance Convoy, Ergnies, France
>
> https://collections.museumvictoria.com.au/items/1954781
>
> Sergeant John Lord, 1916 in Museums Victoria Collections

dog and rabbit

> An unidentified Australian soldier smoking a cigarette while cleaning the mud off an unexploded.
>
> https://www.awm.gov.au/collection/C450191
>
> AWM Accession Number P00308.006

I (into the breech)

> A large quantity of empty shell casings and ammunition boxes
>
> https://www.awm.gov.au/collection/H08331/
>
> AWM Accession Number H08331

without crump

> Shell Blowing Up Railway Line
>
> https://collections.museumvictoria.com.au/items/1706329
>
> Sergeant John Lord, 1916 in Museums Victoria Collections

in turns

> Shells Bursting at Quarry Siding
>
> https://collections.museumvictoria.com.au/items/1706332
>
> Sergeant John Lord, 1916 in Museums Victoria Collections

far and far

> Naval Guns Firing, Quarry Siding
>
> https://collections.museumvictoria.com.au/items/1706356
>
> Sergeant John Lord, 1916 in Museums Victoria Collections

bad luck (for a prayer)

> The devastation on the site of the church in a village destroyed during the Somme Offensive
>
> https://www.awm.gov.au/collection/C46389
>
> AWM Accession Number EZ0096

within the walls (while we lived)

> Australians moving through the ruined village of Voormezeele, near Ypres, Belgium.
>
> https://www.awm.gov.au/collection/C451846
>
> AWM Accession Number E00673

is not

> The village of Flers, on the Somme battlefield.
>
> https://www.awm.gov.au/collection/C43218
>
> AWM Accession Number E00507

residence (lost)

> Damaged City of Lille, During German Occupation
>
> https://collections.museumvictoria.com.au/items/1958241
>
> Museums Victoria Collections

gone (before I sleep)

> A Corner in Albert', France
>
> https://collections.museumvictoria.com.au/items/1703070
>
> Sergeant John Lord, 1916 in Museums Victoria Collections

silent striking

> A road in Albert
>
> https://collections.museumsvictoria.com.au/items/1703705
>
> Sergeant John Lord, 1916 in Museums Victoria Collections

glutton

> Somme, France. 1916. German Army shelters in a canal escarpment. (Donor German War Museum: Bufa 420)
>
> https://www.awm.gov.au/collection/C339805
>
> AWM Accession Number C339805

where we breathe (underground)

> 9th Australian Infantry Battalion camp and graveyard on the Somme, France, ca. 1916
>
> https://www.awm.gov.au/collection/E02021
>
> AWM Accession Number E02021

digging (for victory)

> 24th Battalion at 'Bellewaarde Ridge', Ypres, Belgium, World War I, 21 Sep 1917
>
> https://collections.museumvictoria.com.au/items/2010239
>
> Museums Victoria Collections

again (tomorrow)

> An officer making the daily inspection of his men's feet during the Third Battle of Ypres.
>
> https://www.awm.gov.au/collection/C54942
>
> AWM Accession Number E01120 Hurley, James Francis (Frank), 1917

you can't tell them (back home)

> An unidentified Australian soldier attempting to obtain a drink under a frozen tank.
>
> https://www.awm.gov.au/collection/C54506
>
> AWM Accession Number E00171

the weight of fireworks

> Troops hauling an 18 pounder gun through mud and across shell craters.
>
> https://www.awm.gov.au/collection/C54954
>
> AWM Accession Number E01191

how do I know (unknow)

> View of the swamps of Zonnebeke
>
> https://www.awm.gov.au/collection/C193814
>
> AWM Accession Number H12362

ever (real)

> The war ravaged countryside around Fricourt.
>
> https://www.awm.gov.au/collection/C309958
>
> AWM Accession Number H08394

an eye on the diamantina

> Wounded Soldier, Quarry Camp
>
> https://collections.museumvictoria.com.au/items/1706362
>
> Sergeant John Lord, 1916 in Museums Victoria Collections

wholesome

> WW1 nurses having breakfast, on the verandah at the Aboukir Nurses Rest Home, Egypt, ca. 1915
>
> http://hdl.handle.net/10462/deriv/411546
>
> John Oxley Library, State Library of Queensland Image number: 29854-0010-0001 - Croll, Marion Winifred

fields (of bluebirds)

> Sister Hilda Loxton, a Bluebird, saying adieu to a wounded soldier being evacuated from a mobile hospital.
>
> https://www.awm.gov.au/collection/C271613
>
> AWM Accession Number P01790.003

the devil (to heal)

> A medical orderly, Major Davidson and Sister Lynette Crozier, a Bluebird, applying a dressing.
>
> https://www.awm.gov.au/collection/C271581
>
> AWM Accession Number P01790.001

let us see

> A group of British Army soldiers on the battlefield near Ginchy.
>
> https://www.awm.gov.au/collection/C310398
>
> AWM Accession Number H08452

moments to wonder what

'Men Wounded in the Ypres Battle', 20 Sep 1917

https://collections.museumvictoria.com.au/items/754101

Museums Victoria Collections

on menin mud

After the Battle of Menin Road', Ypres, Belgium, World War 1, 25 Sep 1917 Frank Hurley

https://www.awm.gov.au/collection/C43126

AWM Accession Number E00711 - Hurley, James Francis (Frank), 1917

not dead (enough)

A soldiers' cemetery damaged by shellfire near the town in the Ypres salient.

https://www.awm.gov.au/collection/C355187

AWM Accession Number H13361

too many everywhere we go

Image depicting a memorial cross erected to the 2nd Division at Pozieres Ridge, France.

https://collections.museumvictoria.com.au/items/1707440

Sergeant Major Gilbert P. Mulcahy, Pozreres Ridge, France, 1917. Museums Victoria Collections

laying in arms

Australian Graves at Pozieres', France

https://collections.museumvictoria.com.au/items/1703704

Sergeant John Lord, 1916 in Museums Victoria Collections

no surprises

Two unidentified soldiers look at the inscriptions on the crosses at the cemetery at Vlamertinghe, near Ypres.

https://www.awm.gov.au/collection/C54921

AWM Accession Number E00847

what and who (we breathe)

A dust scene on the Properinghe Road, on the way to Ypres.

https://www.awm.gov.au/collection/C43132

AWM Accession Number E00829

seeing us in (final) trenches

Over the top, a composite shot of a World War I battle in Ypres, Flanders, 1917 Frank Hurley

http://nla.gov.au/nla.obj-138300721

Hurley, Frank. Over the top, a composite shot of a World War I battle in Ypres, Flanders, 1917

weary of

A view, in silhouette, of Australian artillery limbers loaded with ammunition proceeding along the Ypres Road.

https://www.awm.gov.au/collection/C1098

AWM Accession Number E00829

knackered

The 14th Battalion of Australian Infantry resting at Zillebeke in the Ypres Sector.

https://www.awm.gov.au/collection/C954178

AWM Accession Number E00959

ride of the fallen

Artillery horses moving along the tree lined.

https://www.awm.gov.au/collection/C953158

AWM Accession Number E00827

ironic rail

AIF Pioneers building a light railway (or tramway) line.

https://www.awm.gov.au/collection/C384657

AWM Accession Number H16999

perhaps to home

A stretcher party of Australians bringing in wounded along a duckboard track.

https://www.awm.gov.au/collection/C54944

AWM Accession Number E01127

almost (not quite)

The 15th Field Company of Australian Engineers, resting, and playing cards

https://www.awm.gov.au/collection/C1125

AWM Accession Number E01400

Hurley, Frank. Devastated landscape of the Ypres sector, Flanders, 1917

the few (march)

> The road to Ypres becomes the road to Blighty for these infantrymen who have been granted leave.
>
> https://www.awm.gov.au/collection/C953168
>
> AWM Accession Number E00846 - Hurley, James Francis (Frank), 1917

leaving (the somme) now

> Burnt out train carriages in a field at Quarry Siding
>
> https://collections.museumvictoria.com.au/items/1706321
>
> Sergeant John Lord, 1916 in Museums Victoria Collections

to see such heroes

> France, 1916-07. Walking along a road is a group of German prisoners, the first to be captured
>
> https://www.awm.gov.au/collection/C214139
>
> AWM Accession Number C214139

over

> German prisoners from Messines
>
> https://collections.museumvictoria.com.au/items/1700736
>
> Sergeant John Lord, 1916 in Museums Victoria Collections

survived

> Aubrey Lionel Bertram Hampton, a 28-year-old fitter and turner, enlisted on 18 August 1914.
>
> https://collections.museumvictoria.com.au/items/387350
>
> Museums Victoria Collections

taking all

> Puchevillers Cemetery
>
> https://collections.museumvictoria.com.au/items/1706367
>
> Sergeant John Lord, 1916 in Museums Victoria Collections

this field (the river)

> France, 1916-17. One of the water-filled trenches at the Somme during the winter of 1916-17.
>
> https://www.awm.gov.au/collection/C41248 AWM Accession Number P00308.002

touch a place (on the avenue)

> Photograph of the tree planted on the Avenue of Honour, Ballarat, Victoria.
>
> https://www.awm.gov.au/collection/C2143040 AWM Accession Number AWM2016.538.22

Author Information

About the Author

Frank Prem has been a storytelling poet since his teenage years. He has been a psychiatric nurse through all of his professional career, which now exceeds forty years.

He has been published in magazines, online zines, and anthologies in Australia, and in a number of other countries, and has both performed and recorded his work as spoken word.

He lives with his wife in the beautiful township of Beechworth in North East Victoria, Australia.

Connect with Frank

As the author, I hope you enjoyed this volume of poetry collection. I think that mine is a unique style of writing that can appeal well beyond a 'pure poetry' readership.

If you enjoyed it, I'd like to ask you to do two small things for me.

First, take a moment to find your favourite online retail store and leave a short review of the book in your preferred store.

Online reviews provide social proof to readers and are critical to Indie authors such as myself.

The second thing is, please pop over to my author page **www.FrankPrem.com**, and subscribe to receive my occasional Newsletter.

From time to time I'll let you know what is happening with myself and my writing, as well as keeping you informed of any giveaways I may be planning.

You can also find me on Facebook and Twitter.

Other Published Works

Frank Prem

Small Town Kid (2018)

Devil In The Wind (2019)

The New Asylum (2019)

Walk Away Silver Heart (2020)

A Kiss for the Worthy (2020)

Rescue and Redemption (2020)

Pebbles to Poems (2020)

Voices (In the Trash) (2021) – Picture Poetry

The Beechworth Bakery Bears (2021) – Picture Poetry

With Other Authors

Herja, DevastationWith Cage Dunn (2019)

Anthologies

Short Stories of Forest and Fantasy: Fantasy Anthology by OzTales(2019)

Aquarius: Speculative Fiction Inspired by the Zodiac (The Zodiac Series) by Deadset Press

What Readers Say

Small Town Kid

A modern-day minstrel

Highly recommended

—A. F. (Australia)

Small-Town Kid is a wonderful collection

—S. T. (Australia)

A poet's walk through his childhood in a small Australian town.

—J. L. (USA)

Devil In The Wind

Instantly grips you by the throat in his step-by-step story of survival.

Bravo!

—K. K. (USA)

Very moving, beautiful, and terrible

—J. S. (South Africa)

Outstanding!

—B. T. (Australia)

The New Asylum

Brilliant succinct memoir.

__M.P-B. (Australia)

Words can't do justice to the emotional journey I travelled in (reading this collection).

__C. D. (Australia)

If I had to pick one book over the past year that has truly resonated with me, this would be it.

__K. B. (USA)

Walk Away Silver Heart

Has an extraordinary way with words and his poems invoke great passion and emotion in the reader.

—R C (United States)

As Memorable as My Favorite Music

—M D (United States)

Each response becomes a glimpse, and combined, they encapsulate a graceful reflection on a loving relationship.

A beautiful collection.

—D P (United States)

A Kiss For The Worthy

A Celebration of Life Written in Thoughtful Bursts of Poetic Expression

—C M C (United States)

A fascinating poetry collection!

Recommending to true poetry-lovers!

—A N I (United States)

With every verse, I found myself reflecting about myself, my life, and the world.

—K

Rescue and Redemption

The passion of love in its many forms explored by one for another.

—J L (United States)

Refresh your heart and mind

—S C (United States)

I've enjoyed every word, every breath. Every moment within the life of these stories.

—C D (Australia)

Herja, Devastation

Simply written, powerfully felt.

__C. (Australia)

This is a book I will reread and remember for a long, long time.

__C. (Australia)

As a combination of poetry, prose, and wonderfully ominous illustrations, I found Herja, Devastation refreshingly original.

Highly recommended!

—G. B. (Australia)

Index of Individual Poems

FrankPrem.com

CPSIA information can be obtained
at www.ICGtesting.com
Printed in the USA
LVHW011351250621
691051LV00019B/1573